If You Give a Kitty  ...ail

If You Give A Kitty A Cocktail

Written By **Sam Miserendino**

Illustrated By **Mike Odum**

Skyhorse Publishing

Copyright © 2020 by Sam Miserendino

All rights reserved. No part of this book may be reproduced in any manner without the express written consent of the publisher, except in the case of brief excerpts in critical reviews or articles. All inquiries should be addressed to Skyhorse Publishing, 307 West 36th Street, 11th Floor, New York, NY 10018.

Skyhorse Publishing books may be purchased in bulk at special discounts for sales promotion, corporate gifts, fund-raising, or educational purposes. Special editions can also be created to specifications. For details, contact the Special Sales Department, Skyhorse Publishing, 307 West 36th Street, 11th Floor, New York, NY 10018 or info@skyhorsepublishing.com.

Skyhorse® and Skyhorse Publishing® are registered trademarks of Skyhorse Publishing, Inc.®, a Delaware corporation.

Visit our website at www.skyhorsepublishing.com.

10 9 8 7 6 5 4 3 2

Library of Congress Cataloging-in-Publication Data is available on file

Cover and interior artwork by Mike Odum

Print ISBN: 978-1-5107-5066-1
E-Book ISBN: 978-1-5107-5068-5

Printed in China

If You Give A Kitty A Cocktail

Again for Ariel and Sam
-S.M.

Again for Aurora
-M.O

Dedicated To Jason Schneider

Special Thanks To:
Tosca Miserendino
Stacie Odum
Jack W. Perry
Don Loudon
Ron Riffle
Beverly Miserendino
Travis Bundy
Shawn Gates
Joao Pimentel

If you give a kitty
a cocktail,

she couldn't possibly
have another.

Well...if you insist.

And then...

she'll call her friends.

Because everyone knows…

cocktails are better
when shared!

And once they've shared
a cocktail…

Or two…

Or three…

Then the sharing really begins.

Her friends will tell her they always thought she could do better,

because she's the smartest, most beautiful cat they know.

And she'll
believe them.

She'll tell them
she's ready to take
the world by storm!

But first...

She'll have another cocktail.

They all should!
And she will feel so close to her friends,

that she'll start to share…

And share…

And share…

Until, she's interrupted by…

He'll tell her about the places he's been…

The businesses he owns…

The car he
drives…

And he'll tell her…

she's saved by her friends.

When her friends say he seemed sweet at first, it will remind her that it's time for dessert.

They'll tell her they don't have room, unless…
they had one brownie and four forks.

When it's time
to say goodbye,

they all agree they won't wait so long to do this again.

When she wakes up
the next morning,

she'll hope she didn't give him her number…

But she did.

She'll try to remember
everything she said...

But she can't.

When she sees herself in the mirror,
she swears she absolutely, positively will never
have another cocktail in her life.

But a few nights later
when she gets the call,

and she remembers
what a fabulous time
she had…

She will.